PEGGY PORSCHEN

BAKED WITH
LOVE

15 lip-smacking recipes for romantic
cakes, cupcakes and cookies

PHOTOGRAPHY BY
GEORGIA GLYNN SMITH

CONTENTS

Introduction 5

Cookies 6

Cakes 24

Basic Recipes & Decoration 46

Acknowledgments 64

INTRODUCTION

Baked with Love is about sending love to someone special with something that comes from the heart. Baking is love—and often a labor of love—but it's even so much more fun to do if you can create something amazing with your own hands for that special someone. If it then tastes delicious too, well that's just the icing on the cake! I hope you enjoy this little compilation of baked loveliness and that it gives you lots of ideas for your loved ones!

Love,
Peggy x

LUSCIOUS LIPS COOKIES

These cookie kisses make an ideal Valentine's Day gift. The bolder the colors, the better—here I used vibrant reds and pinks.

Divide the royal icing equally between two small bowls. Color one amount of icing with pink food color, the other with red. Add a few drops of water until the icing has reached a soft-peak consistency (see page 50). Fill one pastry bag with each color.

Snip a small tip off each pastry bag and pipe the outlines of the lips in a steady smooth line (see 1 and page 50). Outline red lips with the red icing and pink lips with the pink icing. To prevent it drying out, cover the pastry bags containing the leftover icing with plastic wrap or a damp cloth and put to one side.

Dilute the remaining pink and red icing with a few drops of water until each has reached a flooding consistency (see page 51). Fill one pastry bag with each color and flood the centers of the cookies (see 2), being careful not to overflow at the sides. Let dry.

Once the icing has dried completely, pipe the extra lip detail on each cookie (see 3), using the reserved soft-peak icing. To enhance the lip shape, pipe the detail for the red lips with pink icing and the detail for the pink lips with red icing. Let dry.

MAKES APPROXIMATELY 10–12 COOKIES

Ingredients
10–12 gingerbread cookies in the shape of lips, about 2½in x 4in. (6cm x 10cm), made using 1 recipe quantity of gingerbread cookie dough (see page 47)
14oz. (400g) royal icing (see page 48)
Pink and red food colors

Equipment
Two small bowls
Small icing spatula
Paper pastry bags (see page 49)
Pair of scissors
Plastic wrap or damp cloth

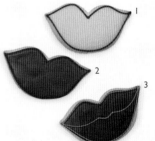

ROSEBUD COOKIES

To complement the rosebud design, I have scented the icing with rosewater. Wrapped in a pretty gift box or cellophane bags, these gorgeous little cookies make an exquisite gift or wedding favor.

Place about 10oz. (300g) of royal icing in a bowl and color it with red food color. Add a few drops of rosewater until the icing has reached a soft-peak consistency (see page 50). Put a small amount of this red icing in a pastry bag.

Snip a small tip off the pastry bag and pipe the outlines for the flowering top of the buds in a steady smooth line (see page 50), leaving enough space for the green leaves at the bottom of the cookies. Pipe all the red outlines first.

Should you have any red icing left over in the bag, squeeze it back into the bowl with the remaining red icing and dilute it with a few drops of rosewater until it has reached a flooding consistency (see page 51). Put this in a fresh pastry bag. Again, snip a small tip off the pastry bag and fill the red-outline centers of the bud heads with the flooding icing, being careful not to overflow at the sides. Let dry.

Once the red icing has dried completely, take about 3½oz. (100g) of icing and color it green and mix to a soft-peak consistency. Put a small amount in a pastry bag, pipe the outline of the stems first, then, as before, make some flooding consistency green icing and flood the centers with that and fill the centers of the stems. Let dry. Reserve a small amount of soft-peak green icing to trace the outline of the stems and leaves later.

Mix the remaining 2oz. (50g) of icing with pink food color to a soft-peak consistency and use to trace the individual petals of the rosebuds. Let dry. Using the reserved soft-peak green icing, trace the outline of the stems and leaves. Let dry.

MAKES APPROXIMATELY 12 COOKIES

Ingredients
12 cookies in the shape of rosebuds, made using 1 recipe quantity of vanilla cookie dough (see page 46)
1lb. (450g) royal icing (see page 48)
Red, pink and green food colors
Small amount of rosewater

Equipment
Several small bowls
Small icing spatula
Paper pastry bags (see page 49)
Pair of scissors
Plastic wrap or a damp cloth

WEDDING CAKE COOKIES

This cookie gives you the option of coordinating the design of your wedding favor with your wedding cake, making a lovely memento for your guests to take home or to send to those who were unable to make it.

Place about 1lb. (450g) of royal icing in a bowl and mix with a little water until the icing has reached a soft-peak consistency (see page 50). Put a small amount of this icing into a pastry bag.

Snip a small tip off the pastry bag and pipe the outlines of the cake shape in a steady smooth line (see page 50). To prevent it drying out, cover the pastry bag containing the leftover icing with plastic wrap or a damp cloth.

Dilute the remaining icing in the bowl with a few drops of water until it has reached a flooding consistency (see page 51). Put this icing in a fresh pastry bag. Again, snip a small tip off the pastry bag and fill the centers with the the flooding icing, being careful not to overflow the sides. Let dry.

Once the icing has dried completely, take about 5oz. (150g) of icing and color it baby-blue and mix to a soft-peak consistency. Place a small amount in a pastry bag. Snip a small tip off the pastry bag and pipe the outline of the bow detail on each cookie. To prevent it drying out, cover the pastry bag containing any leftover icing with plastic wrap or a damp cloth.

Dilute the remaining baby-blue icing with a small amount of water until it has reached a flooding consistency. Put this icing in a fresh pastry bag and use to flood the center of the bow. Let dry.

Using the remaining soft-peak white icing, pipe the outline for the individual cake tiers and a dotted border along the bottom. With the remaining soft-peak baby-blue icing, pipe the detail of the bow. Let dry.

MAKES APPROXIMATELY 6 COOKIES

Ingredients

6 cookies in the shape of wedding cakes (4in. x 5in./10cm x 12.5cm), made using 1 recipe quantity of vanilla cookie dough, see page 46)
1¼lb. (600g) royal icing (see page 48)
Baby-blue food color

Equipment

Small bowl
Small icing spatula
Paper pastry bags (see page 49)
Pair of scissors
Plastic wrap or damp cloth

HEART-SHAPED NAME COOKIES

Turn a simple heart cookie into a stunning decorative feature at the dinner table of a wedding or engagement party. If ribbon is too fiddly, wrap each heart in a cellophane bag and place it on top of each dinner plate. This way your guests can take the cookie home as a personalized keepsake.

As soon as the heart cookies come out of the oven, cut a little hole at the top of each, using the small round cutter. Be careful as the tray will be hot. Let them cool down.

Once the cookies are cold, start with the brown outline. Place about 10oz. (300g) of royal icing in a bowl and color it with a small amount of dark brown food color. Add a few drops of water until the icing has reached a soft-peak consistency (see page 50). Put a small amount of this brown icing into a pastry bag.

Snip a small tip off the pastry bag and pipe the outlines of the hearts in a steady smooth line (see page 50).

Should you have any brown icing left over in the bag, squeeze it back into the bowl with the remaining brown icing and dilute it with a few drops of water until it has reached a flooding consistency (see page 51). Put this in a fresh pastry bag. Again, snip a small tip off the pastry bag and fill the brown-outline centers of the hearts with the flooding icing, being careful not to overflow at the sides. Let dry.

Once the brown icing has dried completely, take the remaining icing and color it with dusky-pink food color and mix to a soft-peak consistency. Put a small amount in a pastry bag and pipe a squiggly outline around the sides of the hearts. Pipe your chosen names or initials in the center. Let dry completely, ideally overnight.

Push a piece of narrow ribbon through the hole and tie into a knot or a bow. Attach to a champagne glass or a napkin to use as a place card.

MAKES APPROXIMATELY 10 COOKIES

Ingredients
10 cookies made in heart shapes (about 2½in./6cm), made using ½ recipe quantity of vanilla cookie dough (see page 46)
12oz. (350g) royal icing (see page 48)
Dusky-pink and dark-brown food colors

Equipment
Small round cutter
Small bowl
Small icing spatula
Paper pastry bags (see page 49)
Pair of scissors
Plastic wrap or damp cloth
1½yd. (1.25m) pastel-pink ribbon, ⅝in.(15mm) width

BRIDE AND GROOM COOKIES

Use these cookies as wedding favors or as a token to accompany your gift to the married couple. To add a personal touch, match the designs to the actual wedding gowns.

Divide the royal icing between two bowls, placing about 9oz. (250g) in one and 12oz. (350g) in the other. Mix the 9oz. (250g) with black food color. Add a few drops of water to both bowls until the icings have reached soft-peak consistency (see page 50). Fill one pastry bag with each color.

Snip a small tip off the pastry bag containing black icing and pipe the outlines of the tuxedos on each groom cookie in a steady smooth line (see 1 and page 50). Using the white icing, pipe the outlines for the shirt and cuffs on the groom cookies and the dresses on the brides.

Dilute the remaining white and black icing with a few drops of water until they have reached a flooding consistency (see page 51). Fill one pastry bag with each color and flood the centers of the cookies in the appropriate colors, being careful not to overflow at the sides. Flood the tuxedo centers with white first (see 2), let dry and then flood the black part (see 3). Let dry.

Once the icing has dried completely, pipe the detail on each cookie, using the remaining soft-peak icing (see 4). Let dry.

MAKES 3 BRIDE AND 3 GROOM COOKIES

Ingredients
3 cookies made in the shape of prom dresses (about 5in. x 4in./12.5cm x 10cm) and 3 cookies in the shape of tuxedos (about 3in. x 4½in./7.5cm x 11cm), made using 1 recipe quantity of vanilla cookie dough (see page 46)
1¼lb. (600g) royal icing (see page 48)
Black food color

Equipment
Two small bowls
Small icing spatula
Paper pastry bags (see page 49)
Pair of scissors
Plastic wrap or a damp cloth

1   2   3   4

MINI HEART FAVORS

Iced heart-shaped cookies are a popular choice for wedding favors. Wrapping the three different shades of pink together in a bag is so pretty. This idea works for any color scheme. Instead of using them as favors, serve them individually as petits fours, arranged on a cake stand or at the side of a coffee cup.

Start with the lightest shade of pink. Place about 3½oz. (100g) of royal icing in a bowl and color it with a tiny drop of pink food color to give a pastel-pink shade. Add a few drops of water until the icing has reached a soft-peak consistency (see page 50). Put a small amount of this pink icing in a pastry bag. To prevent the icing drying out, cover the bowl with plastic wrap or a damp cloth.

Snip a small tip off the pastry bag and pipe the outline of the heart in a steady smooth line (see page 50). Using the pastel-pink icing, outline eight of the heart cookies.

Should you have any pastel-pink icing left over in the bag, squeeze it back into the bowl with the remaining pastel-pink icing and dilute it with a few drops of water until it has reached a flooding consistency (see page 51). Put this in a fresh pastry bag. Again, snip a small tip off the pastry bag and fill the pink-outline centers of the hearts with the flooding icing, being careful not to overflow at the sides. Let dry.

Repeat the above steps, using two darker shades of pink icing, so that you have eight cookies iced in each shade.

If you like, you can pack one of each shade of cookie in a cellophane bag and tie this up decoratively with ribbon.

MAKES 24 COOKIES

Ingredients

24 cookies in small heart shapes (about 1½in./3.5cm), made using ½ recipe quantity of vanilla cookie dough (see page 46)
10oz. (300g) royal icing (see page 48)
Pink food color

Equipment

Small bowl
Small icing spatula
Paper pastry bags (see page 49)
Pair of scissors
Plastic wrap or damp cloth
Eight cellophane bags (optional)
About 5yd. (4m) pink satin ribbon (optional)

MERINGUE KISSES

Pretty pastel-colored mini meringues are simple and yet so adorable; they add a lovely touch to a table for any occasion. Displayed in chic candy jars, they look delicious. With a very long shelf life, they are the perfect gift when wrapped in cellophane bags.

Preheat the oven to 175°F/80°C/gas mark ¼. Line two cookie sheets with parchment or waxed paper.

Place the egg whites and a pinch of salt into the bowl of an electric mixer and start whisking at high speed. Make sure that the bowl is entirely grease-free before you start, otherwise the egg whites will not whip up properly.

As the egg whites are stiffening, slowly sprinkle the superfine sugar into the mix. Stop whisking as the meringue becomes stiffer and glossy; be careful not to overwhisk the mixture.

Add the vanilla extract and slowly fold the confectioners' sugar into the meringue mixture using a rubber spatula.

Separate the meringue mix into three equal parts; keep the first white, mix the second with pink liquid food color to a pastel pink shade and the third with blue and yellow liquid food color for a pastel aqua shade.

Place a star-shaped piping tip in each of the pastry bags then fill each one with a different colored meringue mixture. Pipe little rosettes onto the cookie sheets lined with parchment or waxed paper.

Place the meringues in the preheated oven for between 2–3 hours or until they have fully dried out.

Stored in a dry, airtight container. These mini meringue kisses can last for up to 3 months.

MAKES APPROXIMATELY 100 MERINGUES

Ingredients
3½oz. (100g) egg whites (3 large eggs)
Pinch of salt
½ cup (100g) superfine sugar
1 tsp vanilla extract
Scant 1 cup (100g) confectioners' sugar, sifted
Pink, blue and yellow liquid food color

Equipment
Two cookie sheets
Parchment or waxed paper
Electric mixer
Rubber spatula
Three small bowls
Three large plastic pastry bags
Three star-shaped piping tips
Cellophane bags (optional)

HEART-SHAPED MACARONS

This recipe requires patience and precision. But don't feel put off; once mastered it is so worthwhile. I use my own purple raspberry and rose jam for the filling, but you can create your own flavors.

Preheat the oven to 300°F/150°C/gas mark 2. Cut sheets of baking parchment to fit two large cookie sheets. Using a small heart-shaped cookie cutter or the wide end of a large round piping tip as templates, draw hearts and circles on the reverse side of the parchment at even intervals.

In a food processor, briefly pulse together the ground almonds and confectioners' sugar until mixed well and then sift into a large bowl. Set aside (this is known as a "tant pour tant").

To make an Italian meringue, place the egg whites in a clean, dry bowl. Reserve 1 tablespoon of the egg white to mix with the coloring.

Place the superfine sugar in a small saucepan with the water. Dissolve the sugar over a medium heat, then bring the sugar syrup to the boil. Using a sugar thermometer, measure the temperature of the syrup. When the syrup reaches 240°F/115°C, start to slowly whisk the egg whites. Gradually increase the whisking speed until the eggs are white and frothy. Once the syrup reaches 250°F/120°C, slow down the whisking and carefully pour the hot syrup into the egg whites in a thin steady stream—pour down the side of the bowl so that the syrup does not splash onto the whisk.

Once all the syrup has been incorporated, continue whisking quickly until the meringue has cooled to room temperature; this will take about 5–10 minutes.

Once the meringue has cooled, add your preferred coloring to the reserved tablespoon of egg white and then whisk into the meringue.

MAKES APPROXIMATELY 50 MACARONS

Ingredients
2¼ cups (200g) ground almonds
1¾ cups (200g) confectioners' sugar
7oz. (200g) egg whites
1 cup (200g) superfine sugar
Scant ½ cup (100ml) water
Food color (optional)

Equipment
Two large cookie sheets
Baking parchment
Small heart-shaped cookie cutter
Round piping tip, ½in. (8mm) diameter (I use Wilton No. 12)
Permanent marker pen
Food processor
Two large bowls
Small saucepan
Sugar thermometer
Whisk
Rubber spatula
Plastic pastry bags

Using a rubber spatula, fold the "tant pour tant" into the meringue in three batches. Fold gently but thoroughly to ensure the mix is loose and smooth when piped. The consistency achieved is crucial; the mix should be even and fall easily off the spatula, but not so liquid that it does not keep a good shape when piped. If in doubt, test the mix by dropping a teaspoonful onto the cookie sheet and pulling a peak up on the surface. If it is ready, the top should sink back into the surface gradually. If the peak remains, the mix needs to be folded a little longer.

Place the round tip into the pastry bag. Using a rubber spatula, half fill the pastry bag with macaron mixture. Use a little of the macaron mix to secure the sheets of baking parchment in place on the cookie sheets; smear a small amount of mixture on each corner of the underside of the sheet.

Using the hearts and circles you have drawn as a guide, pipe the macarons. For the hearts, pipe a blob at the top half of the heart and then drag it down to the bottom. Repeat on the other side. If the mixture is the correct consistency, any trails sink back to leave a smooth surface. To finish piping the circles, stop applying pressure to the bag and flick the tip round in a small circular motion as you pull away. This ensures there will be no peak on top of the macaron.

Once the macarons are all piped, gently tap the tray on the work surface to bring any large air bubbles to the surface and pop them with a toothpick. Let the macarons dry out a little on the surface; about 15–30 minutes in dry conditions. You should be able to gently touch the surface of the macaron without your finger sticking.

As soon as the macarons have a dry skin, place them on the lower shelves in the oven and immediately reduce the heat to 275°F/135°C/gas mark 1. If your oven bakes from the top, place a sheet on the shelf above the macarons to prevent the tops from browning too much.

Bake for approximately 15 minutes, turning the sheets halfway through the cooking time. They are done when the tops are dry. Remove the sheets from the oven and transfer the parchment, with the macarons

For a candy stripe swirl, paint three lines of food color down the inside of the tip before fitting it in the bag, filling with mixture and piping.

To make a heart, pipe a blob at the top and drag it downwards. Repeat on the other side.

still attached, directly onto a wet dishtowel. Leave for a few minutes and then remove the macarons. Store in an airtight container at room temperature for up to two days or in the freezer for longer. Sandwich with your chosen filling on the day of consumption, and once filled refrigerate for one hour before eating—this helps the macarons to soften and the flavors to develop.

FLAVORS

Raspberry and Rose Add pink food color to the mixture. When piping, paint the inside of the tip with lines of claret paste food color for a "candy stripe." Proceed as normal with the recipe. Heat the raspberry and rose jam to thicken slightly, let cool, then sandwich with the macarons.

Chocolate Replace ½ cup (50g) of the almonds with ½ cup (50g) cocoa powder, then proceed as normal with the recipe. If desired, add some brown food color to the macaron mixture to get a darker color. Sandwich the shells together with chocolate ganache (see page 54).

TROUBLESHOOTING

Egg whites Separate eggs a few days in advance and leave uncovered in the refrigerator to allow moisture to evaporate and strengthen the whites. Bring egg whites to room temperature before using. To counteract any "watery-ness," add a teaspoon of Meri-White.

Drying If not dried before baking, the tops will not be smooth and produce a good "foot" on the bottom. If dried for too long, they will be smooth but will not produce a foot.

Baking If baked for too long, they will lift easily off the paper but be a bit dry and over-brown; to counteract this, place them in an airtight container in the refrigerator for a day to soften. If not baked enough, they will be too soft and will not lift off the paper.

23

RUFFLE ROSE CUPCAKES

I saw this gorgeously girly cakestand while on a trip to New York, and I just had to have it. Its romantic ruffle design provides the perfect setting for my wild rose cupcakes.

Using the pastry brush, soak the tops of the vanilla sponge cupcakes with the vanilla sugar syrup.

Using a small icing spatula, cover the top of each cupcake with the vanilla buttercream.

Place the marzipan roses and the marzipan leaves on top of the cupcakes, pressing them lightly into the buttercream frosting to fix them in place.

MAKES APPROXIMATELY 25 CUPCAKES

Ingredients
25 vanilla cupcakes, made using ½ recipe quantity basic sponge (see page 52), baked in white paper cases

¾ cup (150ml) vanilla sugar syrup (see page 54)

2¼ cups (500g) vanilla buttercream (see page 55)

75 small dusky-pink marzipan roses (3 per cupcake, see pages 62–63)

150 small moss-green marzipan leaves (6 per cupcake, see pages 62–63)

Equipment
Pastry brush
Small icing spatula

CHOCOLATE HEARTS

French-style chocolate heart cakes make a delightful alternative to chocolates or chocolate truffles. I used an old-fashioned crimping technique for the border design on the monogram heart, which gives this classic design a touch of "retro revival."

Level the top of the heart sponges by trimming off the top crust with a kitchen knife. Gently heat up the apricot jam and brush it thinly all over the little sponges.

On a smooth surface dusted with confectioners' sugar, roll out the chocolate-flavored fondant between the two guide sticks to a piece large enough to cover the top and sides of the cakes. Lay it over them and carefully push it down the sides. Trim any excess fondant off using a kitchen knife.

FOR THE MONOGRAM HEART CAKES

Roll a small amount of chocolate fondant into a thin rope long enough to cover the circumference of eight hearts. Brush the base of each cake thinly with edible glue or clear alcohol and lay the "rope" around the sides.

Gently push the crimping tool all around the base, creating a continuous patterned border.

In a small bowl, mix a small amount of royal icing with pink food color and a few drops of water to produce a soft-peak consistency (see page 50) and put in a pastry bag. Pipe your chosen monogram on top of each cake.

MAKES 24 SMALL CAKES

Ingredients
24 small heart-shaped cakes, made using 1½ recipe quantities of rich dark chocolate sponge (see page 53), baked in miniature heart-shaped baking pans (about 2in./5cm across)
2 tbsp apricot jam, strained
Confectioners' sugar for dusting
About 2¼lb. (1kg) dark-brown chocolate-flavored fondant
Edible glue or clear alcohol (such as vodka)
Small amount of royal icing (see page 48)
Pink food color
About 7oz. (200g) white fondant
Pink edible luster dust

Equipment
Small kitchen knife
Small saucepan
Pastry brush
Rolling pin
Pair of ¼in. (5mm) guide sticks
Serrated crimping tool
Small rolling pin with a lined surface
Paper pastry bags (see page 49)
Pair of scissors
Small heart cutter
Fine artist's brush

FOR THE DOTTED HEART CAKES

Mix the white fondant with a small amount of pink food color. On a plastic board dusted lightly with confectioners' sugar, roll out some of this pink fondant to a strip long enough to cover the base of eight hearts. Roll once over that strip with the lined rolling pin to give it a lined pattern, then cut it into a long strip about ½in. (1cm) wide.

Brush a thin strip around the base of each cake with edible glue or clear alcohol and lay the pink patterned strip around it.

Pipe little dots of pink royal icing all over the top of the cakes. Let dry.

FOR THE HEARTS ON HEART CAKES

On a plastic board dusted lightly with confectioners' sugar, roll out some pink fondant until very thin. Using the small heart cutter, cut out little heart shapes and dust them with pink luster dust.

Brush the back of each heart thinly with edible glue or clear alcohol and randomly arrange the pink hearts all over the cakes. Let dry.

AMERICAN SWEETHEART

Romantically kitsch and sugary sweet, this cake of tiny pink rosebuds and sugar heart motifs couldn't be more girly and appealing. As such, it is perfectly suited to a bridal shower.

Bake and cover the three cakes at least one or two days in advance.

Adjust the scribbler to a measure of about 1in. (2.5cm) and carefully take it around the middle tier as shown (see 1, overleaf) to mark the top limit of the icing border.

Divide the soft-peak royal icing into three and color it two shades of pink and one shade of green. Fill one pastry bag with each color. Place the middle cake tier on top of a piece of parchment or waxed paper and pipe a row of ¾-in. (2-cm) long vertical stripes in alternating colors around the base (see 2, overleaf). Finish each strip with a dot at the bottom and the top. Let dry. Set aside the green-colored icing for later use. To prevent the icing drying out, cover the bowl with plastic wrap or a damp cloth.

Knead the white fondant until it is soft and pliable. Divide it in two and then mix each half with a different amount of pink food color to produce two different shades of pink.

On a plastic board lightly dusted with confectioners' sugar, roll out some of the dark-pink fondant to a long thin strip, trim the edges and cut it into small rectangles about ½in. × 1½in. (1cm × 4cm).

Roll each rectangular strip of fondant into a little rosebud (see 3–5, overleaf). Let them dry. Repeat with the pale-pink fondant. You will need about 250 dark-pink buds and 20 pale-pink buds.

Roll the remaining pale-pink fondant out to a thickness of ¹⁄₁₂in (2mm) and, using the heart-shaped cookie cutter, cut out hearts from it.

MAKES A THREE-TIER CAKE—APPROXIMATELY 70 PORTIONS

Ingredients
3 round sponge cake tiers, 8in. (20cm), 6in. (15cm), 4in. (10cm), made from 3½ recipe quantities of basic sponge, flavored to choice (see page 52), covered with marzipan and then fondant colored pastel pink for top and bottom tiers, and dark pink for the middle tier (see pages 56–58), each set on a matching thick cake board
4oz. (100g) soft-peak royal icing (see pages 50–51)
Pink and green food colors
1lb. 2oz. (500g) white fondant
Confectioners' sugar for dusting
Edible glue or clear alcohol

Equipment
Scribbler
Small bowls
Paper pastry bags (see page 49)
Parchment or waxed paper
Small plastic board
Small rolling pin
Pair of scissors
Small brush
Heart-shaped cookie cutter (about 2in./5cm in diameter)
8 cake dowels
2yd. (1.5m) pink satin ribbon, ½in. (10mm) wide

Lightly mark the bottom cake tier into eight sections radially, like a wheel. Lightly brush the back of each fondant heart with edible glue or clear alcohol (see 6), then stick each one onto the sides of the cake at the outer part of each of the eight sections (see 7).

Using little dabs of royal icing, stick a row of dark-pink rosebuds around the outside edge of each fondant heart (see 8). Arrange the pale-pink rosebuds individually over the middle cake tier and the remaining dark-pink buds in clusters of three all over the top cake tier.

Fill a pastry bag with the remaining green icing. Cut the tip off in a V shape and pipe small leaves around the rosebuds (see 9). Let dry.

Using four dowels each for both the bottom and middle cake tiers, assemble the tiered cake (see pages 60–61).

Trim the bases of the bottom and top tiers with ribbon, securing it in place with a little royal icing.

VALENTINE'S HEART

The romantic floral border cascading down the sides of this cake makes a striking frame for a personal message or someone's name, so it can be used as a billet-doux for any sort of romantic occasion.

Bake and cover the cake at least one day in advance.

Cover the cake board with 5oz. (150g) of the pink fondant and trim with the ribbon (see page 59). Let set overnight.

Using the flower nail lined with pieces of parchment or waxed paper, royal icing and a selection of different piping tips, make a selection of sugar flowers, enough to cover the sides of your cake, as described on page 36. Let dry overnight.

Trim the top crust off both sponges using a serrated knife. Using the 8in. (20cm) heart-shaped cake board as a template, cut two heart shapes out of the sponge.

Soak and layer the two heart-shaped sponges with the flavored sugar syrup and your chosen ganache or buttercream filling (see pages 56–57).

Coat the outside of the cake with the same filling and chill for at least 2 hours. Once chilled, give the cake another coat of ganache or buttercream to make the marzipan stick to the cake.

On a surface lightly dusted with confectioners' sugar, roll the marzipan out between ¼in. (5mm) guide sticks using a large rolling pin.

Using the rolling pin to help you, lay the marzipan over the top of the cake and push it down the sides. Trim away the excess with a knife.

Using the cake smoothers, make the top and sides of the cake nice and even. Let set overnight.

Brush the outside of the marzipan-covered cake with a small amount of clear alcohol to make the fondant stick to the marzipan.

MAKES A 8IN. (20CM) CAKE—APPROXIMATELY 25 PARTY PORTIONS

Ingredients
2 round sponge cakes, 8in. (20cm), made using 2 recipe quantities of basic sponge, flavored to your choice (see page 52)
1⅔lb. (750g) pastel-pink fondant
1¼ cups (300g) royal icing (see page 48)
¾ cup (150ml) sugar syrup, flavored as preferred (see page 54)
Generous 1 cup (250g) filling of your choice, such as chocolate ganache (see page 54) or buttercream (see page 55)
Confectioners' sugar for dusting
1⅓lb. (600g) white marzipan
2 tbsp clear alcohol (such as vodka)
Selection of food colors

EQUIPMENT
12in. (30cm) round or heart-shaped thick cake board
Pink satin ribbon, ⅝in. (15mm) thick
Flower nail
Metal piping tips for petals (Wilton 104, PME 56R, 57R, 58R)
Paper pastry bags (see page 49)
Large serrated knife
8in. (20cm) heart-shaped cake board
Pair of ¼in. (5mm) guide sticks
Pair of cake smoothers
Tilting turntable

Cover the cake with the rest of the fondant following the same technique as for the marzipan (see pages 56–57). Let harden overnight.

Once hardened, pipe a dot of icing in the center of the cake board and place the covered cake on top. Let set for 1 hour so the cake sticks firmly to the board.

Prepare three pastry bags filled with soft-peak royal icing in three different shades of pink.

Place the cake, on its board, on a tilting turntable. Tilt it slightly to the side away from you and then pipe vertical lines down the sides, starting from the top down to the bottom and alternating the three shades (see 1).

Pipe a border of matching dots along the bottom edge (see 2).

Using royal icing, stick the sugar flowers in a heart-shaped frame around the top of the cake, covering the piped lines (see 3).

Fill a pastry bag with green stiff-peak royal icing and pipe green leaves between the flowers, as described on page 33.

PIPING FIVE-PETAL FLOWERS

Cut squares of parchment or waxed paper slightly larger than the flower to be piped. Fit a metal piping tip (Wilton 104 or PME 58R) into a pastry bag. Fill the bag with colored stiff-peak royal icing.

Pipe a small dot of icing on top of the flower nail, stick one of the paper squares on top and hold the nail in one hand.

Hold the pastry bag in the other hand at a 45-degree angle, with the wide end touching the center of the nail and the narrow end pointing out and slightly raised.

Pipe the first petal and give the nail a one-fifth turn as you move the tip out towards the edge. Use less pressure as you move back towards the center and curve the tip slightly to give the petal a natural shape. Stop squeezing as the wide end touches the center of the nail and lift up the tip.

Repeat this four more times to make all the petals.

Remove the flower on its paper from the nail and let dry.

Pipe small yellow dots into the center as stamen.

5-PETAL FLOWERS

DAISIES

PANSIES

DAFFODILS

PIPING DAISIES

Prepare the paper squares and a pastry bag with a tip (Wilton 104) and stiff-peak white royal icing as before.

Mark the center of the paper-lined nail with a dot of icing.

Start at the outer edge of the nail, holding the wide end away from the center and the narrow end towards the center of nail.

Slightly touch the paper with the wide end of the piping tip, squeeze out the icing and pull the tip towards the middle as you release the pressure. Stop and pull the tip away.

Repeat for eight or more petals, while turning nail appropriately.

Finish the flowers as before.

PIPING PANSIES

Prepare two pastry bags with tips of the same size, one filled with yellow and one filled with purple stiff-peak icing.

Using yellow icing, pipe two adjacent petals following the same technique as for the five-petal flower opposite. Repeat and pipe two short yellow petals on top of the large ones.

For the large base petal, using purple icing, tuck the tip under the right side of the large yellow petal and squeeze out a petal the same width as the larger petals, using a back-and-forth hand motion for a ruffled effect.

Remove the flower on its paper from the nail and let dry.

Using a black edible ink pen, draw fine lines in the center of the pansy.

Pipe a fine yellow loop in the middle as a stamen.

PIPING DAFFODILS

Prepare the paper squares and a pastry bag with a tip (PME 58R) and stiff-peak yellow royal icing as before.

Pipe a six-petal flower, using the same technique as for the daisy.

Remove the flower on its paper from the nail and let dry.

Pipe three rings of orange icing on top of each other into the flower center and let dry.

Once dry, pipe a fine ruffled line over the edge of the circle.

Tip: For smaller flowers, simply use smaller piping tips.

ROMANTIC ROSE TOWER

Voluptuous pink roses and gorgeous butterflies "fluttering" on curled wires turn this cake into a piece of pure romance. Inspired by Shakespeare's *A Midsummer Night's Dream*, I designed this cake as a glamorous centrepiece for wedding receptions and engagement parties. It is time-consuming to make, but is well worth the effort. You can make the roses a few weeks in advance, as they keep well. You need to do this at least 3 days ahead and make your marzipan roses and leaves at least 24 hours in advance to ensure they are dry.

Using your round templates, cut out rounds from the sheets of chocolate sponge with diameters graduating from 12in. (30cm) down to 2in. (5cm).

Using a large icing spatula, spread a small amount of chocolate ganache on a 12in. (30cm) cake board and place the 12in. (30cm) round sponge on top.

Spread a thin layer of chocolate ganache over this first cake layer and place the next-largest sponge on top. Continue to assemble the cake layer by layer in this way to form a tapering cone shape.

Cover the whole cake with a thin layer of chocolate ganache and smooth the surface. Place the cake in the refrigerator and let set for at least 2 hours.

Make a triangular paper template that, when rolled, will be large enough to form a cone that will completely cover the cake.

Lightly dust your working surface with confectioners' sugar and roll out the marzipan to a thickness of ¼in. (5mm), using your guide sticks.

Using the paper template, mark and cut out a triangle of marzipan large enough to cover the cake.

MAKES A 12IN. (30CM) CONE-SHAPED CAKE— APPROXIMATELY 120 PARTY PORTIONS

Ingredients
4 sheets of rich dark chocolate sponge (see page 53)
1 recipe quantity chocolate ganache (see page 54)
Confectioners' sugar for dusting
4½lb. (2kg) marzipan
4½lb. (2kg) pink fondant
Small amount of clear alcohol (such as vodka)
About 120 marzipan roses, in different shades of pink, and about 24 marzipan rose leaves (see pages 62–63)
Pink royal icing (see page 48)

Equipment
About 10 round templates with diameters from 2in. to 12in. (5cm to 30cm) for cutting out the cake layers
12in. (30cm) round cake board
Large icing spatula
Large rolling pin
¼in. (5mm) guide sticks
Paper pastry bag (see page 49)
16in. & 18in. (40cm & 45cm) round double cake boards covered with pale pink fondant and deep pink ribbon (see page 59)
Wired feather butterflies

Once chilled, apply another thin coat of chocolate ganache to the cake.

Using your rolling pin, lift the triangle of marzipan and carefully wrap it around the cake. Trim off any excess marzipan from the top and the bottom of the cake. Let it harden overnight.

Next day, following the same procedure as with the marzipan, cover the cake with pink rolled fondant, but instead of using chocolate ganache to stick it on, first brush the cake with the clear alcohol. Let it harden overnight.

Next day, pipe a dot of icing in the center of the double cake board and place the cake on top.

Decorate the cake by sticking the marzipan roses and leaves to the fondant with pink royal icing, starting at the bottom and working upwards (see 1 and 2, left).

Finally, add the wired butterflies to the cake. Stick the wire ends into the marzipan roses evenly over the cake, placing the larger butterflies at the bottom of the cake and the smaller ones at the top.

When serving, make everyone aware that the wired butterflies are not edible, and make sure that they are removed before the cutting and eating of the cake.

TEA ROSE MINI CAKES

Miniature wedding cakes provide a modern twist to the traditional large cake. This particular cake is inspired by the lovely ceramic artistry of the tea set on which it is served. Make the cake at least a day in advance. The flowers can be made well before you need them, as they will last for weeks.

Wrap the soaked sheet of sponge in plastic wrap and chill for about 2 hours until firm. Using 3in. (7.5cm) and 1½in. (3.5cm) round pastry cutters, cut out six rounds in each size from the firmed-up sponge.

Gently heat up the apricot jam and brush it all over the little sponges.

On a smooth surface dusted with confectioners' sugar, roll out the white fondant to ¼in. (5mm) thick using the guide sticks. Cover each of the sponge rounds with the fondant (see pages 56–58).

Use the cake smoothers to straighten the sides and tops of each of the cakes. Trim off any excess fondant using a kitchen knife, place the cakes on a sheet of parchment or waxed paper and let set for a day.

Make the lilac blossoms by mixing the 2oz. (50g) of fondant with a small amount of violet food color. Roll it out thinly on a plastic board lightly dusted with confectioners' sugar. Cut out the lilac blossoms using a mini blossom cutter and shape them with a bone tool. Let dry overnight.

Pipe a small dot of royal icing in the center of each of the large cakes and then place a small cake on top. Pipe a border around the base of each tier and let it dry.

Mix some gold luster dust to a paste with a small amount of clear alcohol and paint the piped border using a fine artist's brush.

Stick the lilac blossoms, mini roses and leaves on top of the cake with little dabs of royal icing.

MAKES 6 MINI CAKES

Ingredients

1 sheet of sponge cake, 12in. × 16in. (30cm × 40cm), made using 2 recipe quantities of basic sponge cake, flavored and soaked as preferred (see page 52)
4oz. (100g) apricot jam, strained
Confectioners' sugar for dusting
18oz. (500g) white rolled fondant
2oz. (50g) white rolled fondant
Violet food color
¼ cup (50g) royal icing (see page 48)
Edible gold luster dust
1 tsp clear alcohol (such as vodka)
About 120 marzipan roses, in different shades of pink, and about 24 marzipan rose leaves (see pages 62–63)
30 mini roses made from dusky-pink fondant (see page 62)
36 rose leaves made from moss-green fondant (see page 62)

Equipment

Round pastry cutters, 3in. (7.5cm) and 1½in. (3.5cm) in diameter
Small rolling pin
¼in. (5mm) guide sticks
Pair of cake smoothers
Small plastic board
Miniature blossom cutter
Bone tool
Paper pastry bags (see page 49)
Fine artist's brush

STRIPEY ROSE MINI CAKES

Smart stripes and candy pink are more fashionable than ever, and help turn these pretty pastries into couture cakes. I recently made these cakes for a friend and, for a change, decorated them with stripes in vivid rainbow colors—they were a great hit. Make these cakes at least a day in advance.

Wrap the soaked and filled sheet of sponge in plastic wrap and chill for about 2 hours until firm.

Using a 2in. (5cm) round pastry cutter, cut out about 15 circles.

Bring the apricot jam to the boil in a small pan and, using a pastry brush, brush each cake all over with the jam.

On a smooth surface lightly dusted with confectioners' sugar, roll out the fondant to ¼in. (5mm) thick using the guide sticks. Cover each cake with the fondant as described on pages 56–58.

Trim off any excess fondant using a small kitchen knife.

Using the cake smoothers, straighten the sides and top of the cakes. Place on a sheet of parchment or waxed paper and let dry for a day.

Once the icing has set firm, fill one pastry bag with soft-peak icing in pastel pink and another with soft-peak icing in bright pink.

Pipe vertical lines as shown, starting at the top in the center, lifting the bag and bringing it slowly down to the bottom of the cake. Touch the end point and stop piping (see page 51). Pipe one line next to the other in alternating colors, keeping the lines nice and straight.

Finish the piped vertical lines by piping small dots in the same colors along the base.

Place a fondant rose on top of each cake and stick it on with a dab of royal icing.

MAKES APPROXIMATELY 15 MINI CAKES

Ingredients

½ sheet of sponge cake, 12in. x 16in. (30cm x 40cm) using 2 recipe quantities of Victoria sponge, flavored, soaked and filled to your choice (see page 52)

⅓ cup (150g) apricot jam, strained

Confectioners' sugar for dusting

1½lb. (750g) white rolled fondant

Generous 1 cup (250g) royal icing (see page 48)

Pink food color

15 pink fondant roses with green calyces (see pages 62–63)

Equipment

Plastic wrap

2in. (5cm) round pastry cutter

Small saucepan

Pastry brush

Small rolling pin

Pair of ¼in. (5mm) guide sticks

Small kitchen knife

Pair of cake smoothers

Parchment or waxed paper

Small icing spatula

Paper pastry bags (see page 49)

VANILLA COOKIES

Line two cookie sheets with parchment or waxed paper.

Place the butter, sugar, vanilla and salt in a mixing bowl and cream together. Do not overwork the mixture or the cookies will spread during baking.

Beat the egg in a measuring cup and slowly add to the butter mixture, whisking until well incorporated. Sift in the flour and mix until just combined. Gather the dough into a ball, wrap in plastic wrap and chill for at least 30 minutes.

Place the dough on a lightly floured surface and briefly knead. Roll out the dough, until about ¼ in. (5mm) thick (unless stated otherwise).

Use cookie cutters to cut out the desired shapes and place the cookies onto prepared cookie sheets. Chill again for about 30 minutes, or until cool and firm. Meanwhile, preheat the oven to 350°F/175°C/gas mark 3.

Bake the cookies for 6–10 minutes, or until the edges are golden brown. Let cool completely on a wire rack.

FLAVOR VARIATIONS

Lemon Omit the vanilla and add the finely grated zest of 1 lemon.

Chocolate Omit the vanilla and replace ½ cup (50g) of the all-purpose flour with ½ cup (50g) cocoa powder.

MAKES 25 MEDIUM OR 12 LARGE COOKIES

Ingredients
1¾ sticks (200g) unsalted butter, softened
1 cup (200g) superfine sugar
Seeds of 1 vanilla bean or 1 tbsp vanilla extract
A pinch of salt
1 large egg, lightly beaten
3 cups (400g) all-purpose flour, plus extra for dusting

GINGERBREAD COOKIES

Line four cookie trays with parchment or waxed paper.

Place the water, brown sugar, molasses, corn syrup, ground ginger, cinnamon and cloves in a deep saucepan. Bring the mixture to the boil over a medium heat, stirring continuously.

Remove from the heat and gradually add the diced butter. Stir until combined. Add the baking soda—take care as the mixture will swell up. Let cool to room temperature.

Once cool, transfer the mixture to a large bowl. Sift in the flour and slowly mix together to form a slightly wet and sticky dough. Wrap in plastic wrap and chill for 2 hours, or until cool and firm.

Place the dough on a lightly floured surface and roll it out, until about ¼ in. (5mm) thick (unless stated otherwise).

Use cookie cutters to cut out the desired shapes and place the cookies onto prepared cookie sheets. Chill again for at least 30 minutes. Meanwhile, preheat the oven to 400°F/200°C/gas mark 6.

Bake the cookies for 8–10 minutes, or until they spring back to the touch and the edges are slightly darkened. Let cool completely on a wire rack.

MAKES 40 MEDIUM OR 20 LARGE COOKIES

Ingredients

5 tbsp water
Generous 1 cup (210g) light brown sugar
3 tbsp molasses
3 tbsp corn syrup
3 tbsp ground ginger
3 tbsp ground cinnamon
1 tsp ground cloves
2¼ sticks (250g) salted butter, cold and diced
1 tsp baking soda
4 cups (560g) all-purpose flour, plus extra for dusting

ROYAL ICING

Place the confectioners' sugar, lemon juice (if using) and three-quarters of the egg white or Meri-White in the clean and grease-free bowl of an electric mixer.

Mix on the lowest speed until well combined. You may want to cover the mixing bowl with a cloth to prevent the confectioners' sugar from going everywhere. If the mixture looks too dry, add more egg white or Meri-White. The icing should look smooth but not wet.

Scrape down the sides of the bowl after about 2 minutes to make sure the icing is well combined. If it still looks too dry and grainy along the edges, add a little more liquid.

If it looks slightly runny and glossy, add a little confectioners' sugar to adjust the consistency.

Continue mixing on the lowest speed for 4–5 minutes, taking care not to overwork or over-aerate the mixture. The royal icing is ready when stiff peaks appear around the sides of the bowl and has a smooth and satin-like texture.

Transfer the royal icing to a clean bowl and cover with a damp cloth. The icing can be stored for up to 1 week at room temperature if covered with a lid or plastic wrap; or in the refrigerator if using fresh egg whites.

MAKES 2¼ LB. (1KG)

Ingredients

8⅓ cups (1kg) confectioners' sugar, sifted
Squeeze of lemon juice (optional)
4 egg whites or 1oz. (25g) Meri-White powdered egg white (mixed with water, as per the instructions on the packet)

COLORING ROYAL ICING

Place the royal icing on a clean smooth surface next to a small amount of paste or liquid food color.

Use an icing spatula to pick up a small amount of royal icing and mix it with the food color. Work the food color through the icing, making sure to break down any tiny specks of color, which can burst and bleed as the icing dries if they are not properly incorporated. Once mixed, gradually add the colored icing to the white icing and blend until you have achieved the required shade.

MAKING A PAPER PASTRY BAG

Take a rectangular piece of parchment or waxed paper or silicone paper—approximately 12in. x 18in. (30cm x 45cm)—and cut it in half diagonally, from 1 corner to the opposite corner. To make a cleaner cut, slide the scissors through the paper rather than making a series of snips.

Hold 1 of the resulting triangles with the longest side at the top, the shortest side to the right and the right-angled corner at the bottom.

Bring the shorter corner down to the bottom corner, turning the paper over on itself to create a cone. With your left hand, wrap the longer corner twice around the cone. Ease the corner towards you so it joins together with the other two corners at the back of the cone.

Manipulate the innermost layer of paper where the three corners meet, pulling it towards you and to the left. Then pull the outermost layer of paper down towards you. Alternate these small movements until the cone forms a sharp point.

Fold the corners at the open end into the inside of the bag. Fold a second time to prevent unravelling.

Only ever half-fill a paper pastry bag with royal icing otherwise the contents will ooze out when you squeeze. Once filled, flatten the open end of the bag with the seam centered on one side. Fold over the two corners at the opening of the pastry bag, then fold over the top of the bag and continue folding until you cannot fold any further; this creates tension that will make piping easier. Always fold away from the seam.

Store filled pastry bags in re-sealable plastic bags until ready to use. When ready to pipe, snip off a small section straight across the top with sharp scissors.

ICING TECHNIQUES

ROYAL ICING CONSISTENCIES

The three useful consistencies of royal icing are stiff-peak icing, soft-peak icing and flooding icing. For soft-peak and flooding consistencies, you simply need to thin down your basic royal icing recipe with water, a little bit at a time, using an icing spatula, until you have reached the right consistency. Always make sure you keep your icing in re-sealable bags when not using, to stop them from drying out.

MAKING STIFF-PEAK ICING

Either use fresh royal icing on the day it is made. Alternatively, place it into a small bowl and mix it through with an icing spatula to loosen and aerate the mixture.

USING STIFF-PEAK ICING

Place the icing into a pastry bag. Snip off a large tip from the point of the filled pastry bag. Pipe along the areas of the cookies you would like to stick together.

MAKING SOFT-PEAK ICING

Dip the icing spatula in water and mix it until the icing looks a little glossy. It should form peaks that fall over.

USING SOFT-PEAK ICING

Place the icing into a pastry bag. Snip off a small tip from the point of the filled pastry bag. Hold the bag between your thumb and fingers; place your thumb over the folded end of the bag so it stays firmly closed, and place your index finger along the seam at the back of the bag. Use the index finger of your other hand to guide the tip.

STIFF-PEAK ICING CONSISTENCY
Used to stick cookies together.

SOFT-PEAK ICING CONSISTENCY
Used to pipe outlines, borders and dots.

FLOODING ICING CONSISTENCY
Used to fill in the center of spaces.

ICING TIPS

- When icing cookies, always outline and flood 1 color at a time, allowing the icing to dry completely before adding the next color to the cookie—unless stated otherwise. This helps to prevent the different colors from bleeding into each other.

- Stronger colors tend to bleed if piped onto paler colors. To avoid bleeding, always ensure that the first color has dried completely before decorating with the second color.

- Outlines in stronger colors tend to be brittle and break easily, so you should make the soft-peak consistency of these colors a little softer than usual. You should also avoid adding too much food color where possible. For example, color royal icing to a charcoal grey shade, which will look black once it dries.

- Flood thin and narrow areas while the outline is still wet, as this will reduce the risk of air pockets that may create holes in the surface when dry.

To pipe lines, hold the bag at a 45° angle to the surface. Touch the starting point with the tip of the bag and slowly squeeze out the icing. As you are squeezing, lift up the bag about 1in. (2.5cm) and guide the line. As you approach the end point of the line, gradually bring down the bag, stop squeezing and drop the line by touching the end point with the tip of the bag.

To pipe dots, hold the bag about 1/32in. (1mm) above the surface and squeeze out the icing to create a dot. Keep the tip low inside the dot and allow the dot to spread to the required size, then stop squeezing and lift off the tip while flicking it in a circular motion. If the dot forms a little peak, flatten it with a damp brush.

MAKING FLOODING ICING

Transfer the icing to a small bowl. Mix with a spatula and add a little water until the icing looks shiny, flows and flattens within 4–6 seconds. Tap the bowl onto a hard surface to bring any air bubbles to the top and prick them with a toothpick. Fill a pastry bag with the icing.

USING FLOODING ICING

Snip off the tip of a filled pastry bag and hold it in your preferred hand. To fill an area, start by flooding just within the soft-peak royal icing border and then continue moving in towards the center. Be careful not to use too much flooding icing, as overfilling can cause the icing to leak and either run off the cookie or into a neighboring color.

When the entire area has been flooded, use a toothpick to push the royal icing into any corners or small sections it hasn't reached. If air bubbles form, you should pop them with a toothpick while the flooding icing is still wet.

BASIC SPONGE CAKE

Preheat the oven to 350°F/180°C/gas 4.

Place the butter, sugar and chosen flavoring in an electric mixer and, using the paddle, cream together until pale and fluffy.

Slowly add the beaten eggs to the mix, paddling on medium speed. If the mixture starts curdling, add a little bit of flour.

Once the eggs and the butter mixture are combined, mix in the flour at low speed.

Line the base and sides of the required baking pan with parchment or waxed paper. For cupcakes, place the cupcake cases into muffin pans. Spread the dough evenly into the pan using a spatula.

Tip: As sponge always rises more in the center, spread it slightly higher around the edge. For cupcakes, fill the paper cases about two-thirds full using a small spoon or a plastic pastry bag.

Bake for 12–15 minutes for cupcakes and 20–45 minutes for large cakes, depending on size. The sponge is cooked when it springs back to the touch and the sides are coming away from the tin. Alternatively, insert the tip of a clean knife into the center; it should come out clean.

Once the sponge is baked, let it rest for about 15 minutes.

Prick the top of the sponge with a wooden skewer and, using a pastry brush, soak it with syrup, while the sponge is still warm.

For cupcakes, wait 10 minutes after baking before soaking with sugar syrup. This way they will not absorb the syrup immediately and seem dry.

Once cool, remove from the pan and continue cooling on a wire rack.

MAKES A 8IN. (20CM) SPONGE, 24 CUPCAKES OR 25 FONDANT FANCIES

Baking temperature: 350°F/180°C/gas 4

Baking time: 12–15 minutes for cupcakes, 20–45 minutes for large cakes, depending on size

Ingredients

1¾ sticks (200g) salted butter, softened

1 cup (200g) superfine sugar

4 large eggs, lightly beaten

1⅓ cups (200g) self-rising flour

½ cup (100ml) sugar syrup (see page 54), flavored as preferred

Optional flavors

Vanilla sponge: add the seeds of 1 vanilla bean

Lemon sponge: add the finely grated zest of 2 lemons

Orange sponge: add the finely grated zest of 2 oranges

Chocolate sponge: replace ½ cup (50g) of flour with cocoa powder and add ½ cup (50g) melted dark chocolate to the butter and sugar mix

Equipment

Basic baking kit, including electric mixer with a paddle attachment

8in. (20cm) cake pan for large cake or fondant fancies, muffin pans and cupcake cases for cupcakes

RICH DARK CHOCOLATE CAKE

Preheat the oven to 325°F/160°C/gas 3.

Line the base and sides of the required baking pan with parchment or waxed paper. For cupcakes place the cupcake cases into muffin pans.

Place the chocolate, milk and half the sugar in a deep pan and bring to the boil, stirring occasionally.

Place the butter and remaining sugar in an electric mixer and cream together until pale and fluffy. Slowly add the beaten eggs.

Sift the flour, cocoa powder, baking powder and baking soda and add to the mixture while mixing at a low speed.

While the chocolate mix is still hot, using a measuring jug, slowly pour it into the dough while mixing at low speed.

Once combined, pour the mix from the bowl directly into the lined pan. For cupcakes, first transfer the cake mix into a jug, as it is very liquid, and fill the cases about two-thirds full.

Bake for 15 minutes for cupcakes and 25–45 minutes for large cakes, depending on size. The sponge is cooked when it springs back to the touch and the sides are coming away from the pan. Alternatively, insert the tip of a clean knife into the center; it should come out clean.

Once the sponge is baked, let it rest for about 15 minutes. Once cool, remove from the pan and cool on a wire rack.

MAKES A 8IN. (20CM) CAKE (HALF TIER) OR 24 CUPCAKES

Baking temperature: 325°F/160°C/gas 3
Baking time: about 15 minutes for cupcakes, 25–45 minutes for large cakes, depending on size

Ingredients
3oz. (75g) dark couverture chocolate drops
3½oz. (100ml) milk
Generous 1 cup (225g) brown sugar
¾ stick (75g) salted butter, softened
2 large eggs, lightly beaten
2 cups (150g) all-purpose flour
1½ tbsp cocoa powder
½ tsp baking powder
½ tsp baking soda

Equipment
8in. (20cm) cake pan for large cake or fondant fancies, muffin pans and cupcake cases for cupcakes

TIP: Bake cupcakes on the day they're iced, as they dry out fast.

TIP: Let sponges rest overnight as they tend to crumble if cut, layered and iced on the same day as baking.

TIP: For storing large sponges, wrap in parchment or waxed paper and then foil, then store in a cool dry place overnight.

TIP: After icing, sponges and cupcakes have a shelf-life of up to 7 days. Wrapped well, the Basic Sponge Cake can be frozen for up to 1 month and the Rich Dark Chocolate Cake up to 3 months.

SUGAR SYRUP

Place the water or juice and sugar in a deep pan and bring to a boil. Remove from the heat and allow it to cool.

Once cool, stir in the flavorings.

Ideally, let the syrup infuse overnight as this brings out the flavors most effectively.

If kept in an airtight bottle or container and refrigerated, it lasts for up to 1 month.

MAKES ½ CUP (100ML)
Roughly the amount needed for a 8in. (20cm) cake tier, a 12in. (30cm) single tier square sponge, 25 fondant fancies, or 24 cupcakes.

Ingredients
for vanilla syrup
5 tbsp water
⅓ cup (75g) sugar
Seeds from ½ vanilla bean or 1 tsp Madagascan vanilla essence

for lemon syrup
5 tbsp freshly squeezed lemon juice
⅓ cup (75g) sugar
1 tbsp Limoncello liqueur
for orange syrup
5 tbsp freshly squeezed orange juice
⅓ cup (75g) sugar
1 tbsp Grand Marnier liqueur

Equipment
Deep saucepan
Spatula

CHOCOLATE GANACHE

Place the chocolate drops in a bowl. Place the cream in a saucepan, stir well and heat it up to a bare simmer.

Pour the hot cream over the chocolate and whisk together until smooth. Don't over-whisk the ganache, as it can split easily.

Cool slightly until just setting before use. It can be stored in a sealed container in the refrigerator for up to 1 month.

MAKES 2½ CUPS (500G)
Roughly the amount needed to layer a 8in. (20cm) cake tier

Ingredients
10oz. (250g) dark couverture chocolate drops (minimum 53% cocoa)
1¼ cups (500ml) light cream

Equipment
Heatproof mixing bowl
Saucepan
Whisk

BUTTERCREAM FROSTING

This frosting uses equal quantities of butter and confectioners' sugar and, as it is egg-free, has a longer shelf-life than other buttercreams.

Place the butter, confectioners' sugar, salt and flavoring in the bowl of an electric mixer and, using the paddle attachment, bring the mixture together on low speed. Turn the speed up and beat until light and fluffy.

If not using immediately, store in a sealed container in the refrigerator and bring it back to room temperature before use. If refrigerated, it has a shelf-life of up to 2 weeks.

MAKES 2½ CUPS (500G)
Roughly the amount needed to layer a 8in. (20cm) cake tier.

Ingredients
2½ sticks (250g) unsalted butter, softened
1½ cups (250g) confectioners' sugar, sifted
Pinch of salt

Optional flavors
Vanilla: add the seeds of 1 vanilla bean
Lemon: add the finely grated zest of 2 lemons
Orange: add the finely grated zest of 2 oranges
Strawberry: add 2 tbsp good strawberry jam and a tiny drop of pink food color

Chocolate: replace half the buttercream with chocolate ganache (see page 54)
Mocha: add a double shot of cool espresso to the chocolate buttercream

Equipment
Electric mixer with a paddle attachment

LAYERING AND ICING CAKES

Tiered cakes, as well as miniature cakes, provide the option of mixing different flavors of cakes. If you would like to make a tiered cake with different flavors, you have to bear in mind that the bottom tier has to carry the weight of the other tiers and therefore a stronger cake base should be used for the bottom tiers and lighter cakes for the top. For example, if you use my recipes, I recommend using chocolate cake for the lower tiers and the lighter basic sponge-based cakes for the upper tiers.

Using a cake leveller or large serrated knife, trim the top and bottom crusts off both sponges.

Slice each sponge in half so you have four layers of the same depth (about 1in./2cm each).

Place the cake board on the turntable and spread with a thin layer of buttercream or ganache. Put the first sponge layer on top and soak with sugar syrup if required (see 1).

Spread the sponge with buttercream or ganache, put the second sponge layer on top (see 2). Soak with sugar syrup.

Keep on layering the remaining pieces of sponge in this way with preserves, buttercream or ganache until all four layers are assembled. Press the layers down gently but firmly to ensure that the cake is level (see 3).

Using a large icing spatula, coat the outside of the cake with buttercream or ganache (see 4). Start spreading from the top center and towards the edge as you rotate the turntable.

Push the buttercream down the sides and spread it evenly all round the sides.

Use a metal side scraper to clean up the sides (see 5) and do the same on the top with an icing spatula.

MAKES ONE 8IN. (20CM) ROUND CAKE TIER

For a 8in. (20cm) round cake tier you need two 8in. (20cm) round sponges.

Ingredients

Two 8in. (20cm) sponge cakes (see pages 52 and 53)

for the filling:

About 2 cups (600g) buttercream flavored to choice (see page 55), chocolate ganache (see page 54), jam, marmalade or lemon curd

About 1 cup (200ml) sugar syrup (see page 54), flavored to choice (for basic sponge only)

Confectioners' sugar for dusting

About 2¼lb. (850g) marzipan

Small amount of clear alcohol (such as vodka)

About 2¼lb. (850g) rolled fondant icing

Equipment

Cake leveller or large serrated knife

Small kitchen knife

8in. (20cm) round cake board

Large icing spatula

Pastry brush

Metal side scraper

Turntable

Confectioners' sugar sifter

Large rolling pin

Pair of guide sticks

Pair of cake smoothers

Scriber

Chill for at least 2 hours or overnight until the cake has set and feels firm.

Once set, dust a working surface with confectioners' sugar, place marzipan on it and, using guide sticks, roll out to an even round large enough to cover the top and sides.

Lift the marzipan with the rolling pin, lay it over the cake (see 6) and gently push it down the sides. Trim off any excess marzipan using the kitchen knife.

Polish the marzipan with the cake smoothers (see 7) and use the palms of your hands to smooth the edges. Let the marzipan dry, preferably overnight.

Once set, brush the marzipan with a thin coat of clear alcohol to stick on the fondant icing. The alcohol not only destroys any bacteria that may have built up while storing the cake, but it also evaporates within minutes after its application and therefore creates a strong and hygenic glue between the marzipan and the fondant. Should you prefer not to use alcohol, use boiled cold water instead.

Apply the fondant layer in the same way as the marzipan layer (see 8).

CAKE AND FILLING COMBINATIONS

Vanilla sponge, soaked with vanilla syrup, layered with raspberry preserve and vanilla buttercream

Lemon sponge, soaked with lemon and Limoncello syrup, layered with lemon curd and lemon buttercream

Orange sponge, soaked with orange and Grand Marnier syrup, layered with luxury orange marmalade and orange buttercream

Rich dark chocolate cake layered with Belgian chocolate ganache

Vanilla sponge, soaked with morello cherry jam

Rich dark chocolate cake layered with vanilla buttercream and mocha buttercream

Lemon sponge layered with vanilla, strawberry and chocolate buttercream

COVERING CAKE BOARDS

Dust the cake board thinly with confectioners' sugar and brush it with a little alcohol (to make a glue for the fondant).

Roll the fondant out to about ⅛in. (3mm) thick and large enough to cover the cake board.

Use the rolling pin, lift the fondant and lay it over the board (see 1).

Let the cake smoother glide carefully over the surface of the fondant and push out any air bubbles.

Lift the board with one hand and push the fondant down the side with the smoother in the other hand (see 2).

Trim the excess fondant off with a sharp kitchen knife (see 3) and let it dry for 1 to 2 days.

Once the fondant is dry, wind the ribbon around the edge of the board and fix the ends with a metal pin.

Ingredients
Confectioners' sugar for dusting
Small amount of clear alcohol
   (such as vodka)
Rolled fondant icing

Equipment
Thick cake board of the required
   size
Pastry brush
Rolling pin
Cake smoother
Small kitchen knife
⅝ in. (15mm) wide satin ribbon
   to cover the sides

ASSEMBLING TIERED CAKES

Using a large spatula, spread the center of the iced board with a thin layer of royal icing that doesn't exceed the size of the bottom tier.

Carefully lift your bottom tier with the spatula and center it on top of the cake board (see 1).

Using a template, mark positions for 4 dowels and push dowels down into the cake (see 2). They stop upper tiers sinking into lower ones.

With a food color pen, mark each dowel about ½in. (1cm) above the point at which it comes out of the cake.

Carefully remove the dowels, line them up next to one another and cut to the same length, using the average mark as a guide line. Stick them back in the cake. To see if they all have the same height, place a cake board on top of them and check that it sits straight, ideally using a small spirit level. Should you have to readjust the length of a dowel, carefully pull it out of the cake with tweezers and trim it with scissors then replace.

Once happy with the dowels, spread a little icing in the middle of the cake, carefully lift the second tier with your spatula and center it on top of the bottom tier.

Repeat these steps for second and third tiers if required (see 3).

Once all your tiers are assembled, mix the fondant with water to a thick but smooth paste. Put in a paper pastry bag and squeeze into the gaps between tiers to fill them.

Dampen your finger with a damp cloth and run it along the filled gaps to wipe off excess fondant (see 4).

Tip: Depending on transportation and distance to the event, it may be safer to assemble a tiered cake on site.

Ingredients

Cake tiers of different sizes, covered with marzipan and fondant
Iced cake board about 3–4in. (7–10cm) larger than the bottom tier
Royal icing (see page 48)
Small amount of fondant the same color as the icing
Small amount of water

Equipment

Plastic dowels (4 for each tier except the top one)
Large spatula
Serrated kitchen knife
Pair of strong scissors
Food color pen
Dowel template
Paper pastry bag (see page 49)
Small bowl
Damp cloth
Spirit level
Pair of tweezers

MARZIPAN ROSES

To make a rosebud, you need two hazelnut-sized balls of dark pink marzipan and one twice as large. Place these pieces of marzipan between two sheets of cellophane (see 1) and, starting with the larger one, push it down sideways to make it longer, and then flatten one long side with your thumb until very thin (see 2).

For the other petals, push a smaller ball down with your thumb, starting from the center to one side, until it forms a round petal with one thick and one thin side. Repeat with the other.

Roll the large petal to a spiral shape, thin side up (see 3). This will form the center of the rose. Take one of the smaller petals, thin side up, and lay it around the center over the seam (see 4). Tuck the third petal slightly inside the second and squeeze it around the center (see 5). Slightly curve the petal edges out with your fingertips (see 6).

To make small roses, continue by laying another three petals of the same size around the rosebud, each slightly overlapping. Again, slightly curve the edge of the petals out with your fingertips.

To make large roses, continue by laying another five petals of the same size around the rosebud, each slightly overlapping. Slightly curve the edge of the petals out with your fingertips.

To finish, pinch any excess marzipan off the bottom (see 7).

To make calyces and leaves, roll out some green marzipan between the two sheets of cellophane. Cut a calyx out with the rose calyx cutter and stick it underneath the bottom of the rose (marzipan will stick to itself; for fondant use a little bit of water).

Pinch and shape the tips with your fingers as required.

Cut the leaves out with the rose leaf cutter. Press in the rose leaf veiner (see 8) and shape with your fingers for a natural look (see 9).

MAKES ABOUT 6 LARGE OR 12 SMALL ROSES OR 20 ROSEBUDS

Ingredients
9oz. (250g) neutral marzipan (you can use fondant instead)
Pink food color
Green food color

Note: color two-fifths of the marzipan pale pink, two-fifths dark pink and one-fifth green

Equipment
2 sheets of cellophane
Small rolling pin
Rose calyx cutter
Rose leaf cutter
Leaf veiner

ACKNOWLEDGMENTS

Since there is so much love in this book, I thought it's about time to give back some love and say a HUGE THANK YOU to all my loyal fans and readers that have been supporting me over the past 10 years since I wrote my first book! I am truly touched by how enthusiastic and encouraging so many cake fans feel about my work and it's what keeps me excited and inspired.

Hugs & Kisses,
Peggy X

Publishing director Sarah Lavelle
Commissioning editor Lisa Pendreigh
Creative director Helen Lewis
Designer Emily Lapworth
Photographer Georgia Glynn Smith
Production director Vincent Smith
Production controller Stephen Lang

This edition published in 2017 by
Quadrille Publishing Ltd
www.quadrille.com

Text, recipes and designs © 2014 Peggy Porschen
Photography © 2014 Georgia Glynn Smith
Artwork, design and layout © 2014 Quadrille Publishing

The rights of Peggy Porschen to be identified as the author of this work have been asserted by her in accordance with the Copyright, Design, and Patents Act 1988.

British Library Cataloguing-in-Publication Data
A catalogue record for this book is available from the British Library.

ISBN: 978 178713 046 3
Printed in China

A selection of the cutters, stencils and moulds used in this book are available from peggyporschen.com

The cookie dimensions in the book all use the formula width x height.